A CULTURAL HISTORY OF WOMEN IN AMERICA

WOMEN CLAIM THE VOTE: THE RISE OF THE WOMEN'S SUFFRAGE MOVEMENT 1828–1860

CATH SENKER

Clifton Park - Halfmoon Public Library
475 Moe Road
Clifton Park, New York 12065

CHELSEA HOUSE
An Infobase Learning Company

WOMEN CLAIM THE VOTE: THE RISE OF THE WOMEN'S SUFFRAGE MOVEMENT 1828–1860

Copyright © 2011 Bailey Publishing Associates Ltd

Produced for Chelsea House by Bailey Publishing Associates Ltd, 11a Woodlands, Hove BN3 6TJ, England

Library of Congress Cataloging-in-Publication Data
Senker, Cath.
  Women claim the vote : the rise of the women's suffrage movement, 1828-1860 / Cath Senker.
    p. cm. — (A cultural history of women in America)
  Includes index.
  ISBN 978-1-60413-930-3
  1. Women—United States—Social conditions—19th century—Juvenile literature. 2. Women—Suffrage--United States—History—Juvenile literature. 3. Feminism—United States—History—19th century—Juvenile literature. 4. United States—Social conditions—19th century—Juvenile literature. I. Title. II. Series.
  HQ1418.S46 2011
  324.6'23097309034—dc22
                        2010045960

Project management by Patience Coster
Text design by Jane Hawkins
Picture research by Shelley Noronha
Printed and bound in Malaysia
Bound book date: April 2011

10 9 8 7 6 5 4 3 2 1   3196
This book is printed on acid-free paper.

The publishers would like to thank the following for permission to reproduce their pictures:
akg-images: 11, 20 (IAM), 21, 23 (historic-maps), 32, 36, 42, 54; akg/North Wind Picture Archives: 5, 10, 13, 15, 29, 40, 41; The Art Archive: 38, 59 (Culver Pictures); Corbis: 9 (The Stapleton Collection), 28 (Bettmann), 34 (Bettmann), 39 (Bettmann), 44 (Bettmann), 53 (Lake County Museum), 55 (Bettmann), 57 (Bettmann); Getty Images: 8, 12, 14, 31, 45, 52; Lebrecht Music & Arts/North Wind: 22; The Library of Congress: 35, 46; Mechanics Hall, Worcester, MA: 47; TopFoto/The Granger Collection: 6, 7, 16, 17, 18, 19, 24, 25, 26, 27, 30, 33, 37, 43, 48, 49, 50, 51, 56, 58.

CONTENTS

Introduction   5

Chapter 1: An Era of Change   6

Chapter 2: Home and Daily Life   10

Chapter 3: Working Life   18

Chapter 4: Women's Organizations   26

Chapter 5: The Abolitionist Movement   34

Chapter 6: Claiming the Vote   42

Chapter 7: Education and the Media   50

Chapter 8: The Period in Brief   58

Timeline   60

Glossary and Further Information   62

Index   64

IN 1828, IT WAS CONSIDERED IMPROPER FOR American women to speak in public, preach, or work in most professions. Legally, a married woman belonged to her husband and had no control over her property or wages. Women could not vote, hold public office, or serve on juries.

Among the white middle class, the ideology of "separate spheres" held sway. Girls and women stayed home, while men were responsible for paid work and business outside the home. The idea of separate spheres was reinforced with the beginning of industrialization and the growth of waged jobs, mainly taken by men. Nevertheless, women did work alongside men on farms and in family businesses.

The separate spheres ideology was not universal. In poor white families, all family members worked. Enslaved African Americans, both male and female, undertook hard physical labor. According to traditional customs, Native American women held authority in their communities through their control over the home and food production.

Right: A woman sewing at home in the 19th century. In this illustration, the young woman looks relaxed; sewing was one of the less strenuous tasks of an American housewife.

FOOL'S PARADISE?

"While woman's intellect [ability to think] is confined, her morals crushed, her health ruined, her weaknesses encouraged, and her strength punished, she is told that her lot is cast in the paradise of women: and there is no country in the world where there is so much boasting of the 'chivalrous' [honorable] treatment she enjoys. That is to say,—she has the best place in stagecoaches [carriages pulled by horses]: when there are not chairs enough for everybody, the gentlemen stand: . . . her husband's hair stands on end at the idea of her working, and he toils to indulge her with money. . . . In short, indulgence is given her as a substitute for justice."

British author Harriet Martineau published *Society in America* (1837) after her travels in the United States. Here she says that "chivalry" toward women (she implies white women) restricts their opportunities.

AN ERA OF CHANGE

URING THE FIRST HALF OF THE 19TH CENTURY, the Industrial Revolution began to transform the American economy. In the South, the cotton gin sped up cotton production, while in the North, large textile mills sprang up. From the 1830s, railroads were constructed. At the same time, many people abandoned farming and moved to the growing towns and cities to seek work. Jobs opened up for men as store workers, merchants, or lawyers. By 1860, New York City was home to one million people, while Philadelphia had 500,000 inhabitants.

TURNING POINT

THE INDUSTRIAL REVOLUTION IN AMERICA

Eli Whitney invented the cotton gin, a machine for cleaning the seeds from cotton, in 1793. It made cotton production much faster. During the first half of the 19th century, cotton gins spread throughout the South. Slaves operated the machines. Steam-powered spinning and weaving equipment had been invented in England in the late 18th century. In the 1810s, Francis Cabot Lowell toured British textile factories, memorized the design of textile machines, and then began to establish textile mills in the United States. After Lowell died in 1817, his colleagues set up the Lowell factory town. The textile factories helped to expand the Industrial Revolution.

Right: Women slaves operate a cotton gin, a device that pulled the cotton through a set of wire teeth to remove the seeds. The invention made slavery even more important to the southern economy because large numbers of laborers were required to work the machines.

Above: The De Witt Clinton steam locomotive, 1831, was one of the earliest trains and the first locomotive built in New York. The passenger coaches resembled horse-drawn stagecoaches.

THE SOUTH AND SLAVERY

In the South, the economy remained based on agriculture, mainly cotton, tobacco, and sugarcane production. Whereas in the North, slavery had been abolished by the 1820s, the South was dependent on slave labor for its economic success. Enslaved African Americans were forced to work on plantations from sunup to sundown and could be punished or sold at the will of their master.

MOVES TOWARD ABOLITION

From the 1820s to 1850s, slavery increasingly caused division within the country. Most white Americans accepted slavery in the South, but the southern states wanted to expand slavery into the western territories, such as Kansas and Nebraska, where pioneers were starting to settle. Southerners argued that slaves were property and that people should be able to bring their property with them. Many northern politicians did not want slavery to spread westward, and an abolitionist movement was growing among northerners.

FREE BLACK PEOPLE

Although free African Americans in the North had a better life than slaves, they suffered from discrimination. Some states had segregation laws. For example, black people were forbidden

BREAKTHROUGH BIOGRAPHY

MARIA WESTON CHAPMAN (1806–85)

Born in Weymouth, Massachusetts, Maria Weston was sent to England to receive a good education. She returned to the United States and married businessman Henry Chapman in 1830; they had four children. Maria helped to found the Boston Female Anti-Slavery Society in 1832 and ran anti-slavery fairs to raise funds for the movement. She was also involved in the wider abolitionist movement and supported radical William Lloyd Garrison, who argued that all slaves should immediately be freed. In 1840, Maria was selected to join the executive committee of the American Anti-Slavery Society. After her youngest daughter and her husband died of tuberculosis in 1842, she traveled to Europe with her surviving three children and gathered support for the anti-slavery campaign. The family returned to the United States in 1855, and Maria continued her abolitionist mission. Her active leadership in the movement challenged people's expectations of women at the time.

Above: An African-American preacher addresses a mixed congregation on a plantation in South Carolina in 1863. Slaves also held their own secret meetings where they prayed for freedom from bondage.

to enter many public buildings and spaces or to use public buses. Separated from white society, northern black people organized their own churches and self-help groups to support their communities.

RELIGIOUS LIFE

Religion was at the core of all communities, black and white. Many different churches existed, including the Catholic Church; various Protestant sects, including the Puritans and Methodists; and the Quakers. Large numbers of people attended church regularly—especially women. Women were taught to live according to religious morals and be obedient to men; they were seen as more virtuous than the opposite sex.

A religious revival movement, the Second Great Awakening, had begun in 1790 and continued through the 1840s. Many people attended revivals and camp meetings, and the number of people joining churches increased. As part of the movement, ministers encouraged their followers to help the needy, which led to an upsurge in enthusiasm for charitable and reform groups that worked to improve society.

LAND AND GOLD

The acquisition of vast swathes of territory in the 1840s transformed the United States. White settlers moved to seek farmland. The discovery of gold in 1848 in the new territory of California led to "gold fever." Many people traveled to California, hoping to make their fortune from the gold mines. But the westward expansion had a devastating effect on the Native Americans and Mexicans already living in those regions.

Below: In this illustration from the war with Mexico, U.S. troops storm the Bishop's Palace in Monterrey, Mexico, in 1846. Monterrey was the capital of a large region that included all of modern-day California. The United States won the battle and claimed the area.

TURNING POINT

WAR WITH MEXICO, 1846–48

Between 1800 and 1850, the U.S. population grew rapidly from over five million to more than twenty-three million, so Americans wanted to acquire additional territory. Meanwhile, Mexico had won vast lands from Spain in its war of independence in 1821. But the Mexican government proved unable to extend its authority over the new area. In 1845, the United States annexed (took control of) the Mexican state of Texas. In 1846, it took over Oregon south of 49 degrees north latitude through a treaty with Britain. In the same year, the United States hoped to acquire California from Mexico. This time, Mexico decided to fight. The United States won the war and gained over 500,000 square miles of Mexican territory—the present Southwest, from Texas to California.

CHAPTER 2

HOME AND DAILY LIFE

EXCEPT FOR A MINORITY OF WEALTHY WOMEN WHO COULD afford servants to do all the housework and child care, most women led exhausting lives. Domestic work in the mid-19th century was extremely time consuming. Women and girls had to bring in all the water they needed for washing and cooking and tend to an open fire or wood-burning stove to heat water and cook. Doing the laundry took an entire day. Some issues were common to all women, although their experiences varied depending on their class, race, and location.

THE WORKING WEEK

"*Monday, with some of the best housekeepers, is devoted to preparing for the labors of the week. Any extra cooking, the purchasing of articles to be used during the week, and the assorting of clothes for the wash, and mending. . . . Tuesday is devoted to washing, and Wednesday to ironing. On Thursday, the ironing is finished off, the clothes folded and put away, and all articles which need mending put in the mending basket, and attended to. Friday is devoted to sweeping and housecleaning. On Saturday, and especially the last Saturday of every month, every department is put in order for Sunday. All the cooking needed for Sunday is also prepared.*"

In *A Treatise on Domestic Economy*, by Catharine E. Beecher, published in 1841, the author advises her middle-class readers how to organize their week.

Right: A woman working with a spinning wheel. Most women still made all the family's clothes. They spun thread from wool or cotton and wove it into fabric using a hand loom.

HEALTH

In addition to undertaking housework, women nursed sick family members, including youngsters with childhood diseases and elderly relatives. Poor health was a constant worry. Medical

Above: Jonathan Eastman Johnson based this 1859 painting, *Old Kentucky Home,* on his observations of slave quarters in Georgetown, Washington, D.C.

knowledge was limited, and physicians had little idea of how to cure disease. Most popular antebellum (pre-Civil War) treatments involved "heroic" medicine—methods that caused a significant reaction in the body. These included leeching (letting leeches suck out blood) and bloodletting. Such treatments often made the patient worse. There was no awareness of the importance of hygiene, so people with a mild disease or injury often died from infections.

CHILDBEARING

Women in America commonly had several children; farming families wanted plenty of hands to help on the farm. The majority of married women spent most of their lives being pregnant or nursing babies. Yet women would have welcomed a break from childbearing. Also, having babies was a dangerous business. Virtually all women gave birth at home with little or no medical help. There were few hospitals, and those that existed were generally dirty.

Birth control was rarely practiced in the early 19th century, but by mid-century, a growing number of couples, especially in the urban

TURNING POINT

A CHOLERA EPIDEMIC

In June 1832, cholera hit New York City. About 3,000 people died before the epidemic began to slow down in September. The city already had a Board of Health, but previously it had been individuals, charities, and other groups that had responded to health emergencies. For the first time, the New York City Board of Health took the lead in responding to the disease. It built temporary hospitals, moved people out of the worst slums, and paid for the garbage-filled streets to be cleaned. The Board's decisive actions provided the basis for a more organized, government-led response to health issues later in the century.

Above: A depiction of a middle-class family in the mid-19th century. Middle-class families had large homes; even with servants, there was much work to do to run them. In this period, standards of housekeeping rose, and women spent a large amount of time keeping up the home. They were expected to have the best furnishings, all maintained in good condition.

BREAKTHROUGH BIOGRAPHY

FRANCES WRIGHT (1795–1852)

Frances Wright was born in Scotland. Her parents died when she was a child, and she left to live with relatives in London. Frances went to the United States in 1818, where she developed her radical ideas. She was horrified by slavery and believed in equal relationships between men and women. In 1825 she founded a commune called Nashoba to try to put her ideas into practice. She intended slaves to join and work toward their freedom, but the experiment failed. In the 1830s Frances devoted herself to campaigning for social change. She believed in a radical overhaul of society, with the government providing jobs for everybody and a more equal distribution of property. Frances focused on women's rights, including the need for birth control and the easing of divorce laws. She had little support, and other women's rights activists attacked her extreme views. Yet her opinions helped to challenge assumptions about womanhood.

Northeast, were starting to limit family size. Whereas the average number of live births had been just over seven in 1790, by 1850 the number of live births for an average woman was around five.

WHITE WOMEN

Women's experiences varied according to race. The best opportunity for a young white woman was to marry a well-off husband and raise a family. Women seldom had a college education or paid job, so found it hard to be independent. Most single women had to remain living with their family.

FAMILY LIFE

Raising children was considered the mother's responsibility. This improved the status of middle-class women, especially the influence they had over their sons. Mothers were expected to instill values in their sons that would make them successful in later life.

DIVORCE

If marriage and family life did not work out, a couple might want a divorce. Absolute divorce allowed the former spouses to remarry, while legal separation enabled them to live apart but not to remarry. However, few reasons for divorce were accepted, and the legal costs were high. Generally, it was much harder to end a marriage in the South. Most unhappily married women remained with their husband anyway because they could not survive alone financially. During the antebellum period, legal reforms gradually made it easier to secure a divorce, and the number of divorces granted to couples increased.

WHITE WOMEN IN THE SOUTH

White women in the South tended to have even fewer opportunities than their northern counterparts. Most were in farming families. Living conditions were often poor: many families inhabited log cabins, with unglazed windows and the

---

Below: Pioneers build a log cabin. These were typically one-story structures built as the first shelter in a frontier area. Here the woman cooks while the men labor, but women usually helped with the construction work.

LIVING CONDITIONS

"Nine times out of ten, at least . . . I slept in a room with others, in a bed which stank, supplied with but one sheet, if with any; I washed with utensils common to the whole household; I found no garden, no flowers, no fruit, no tea, no cream, no sugar, no bread . . . no curtains, no lifting windows (three times out of four absolutely no windows), no couch—if one reclined in the family room it was on the bare floor—for there were no carpets or mats. For all that, the house swarmed with vermin. There was no hay, no straw, no oats (but moldy corn and leaves of maize), no discretion, no care, no honesty."

Frederick Law Olmsted, the designer of New York's Central Park, traveled through the southern states in the 1850s. He found that poor white farmers lived in miserable conditions, little better than those of slaves. Here he describes a typical home in the area between the Mississippi and the Upper James rivers.

"

PLEASE BUY ALL OF US

"Massa Black am awful cruel and he whip de cullud folks and works 'em hard and feed dem poorly. . . . We'uns have to work in de field every day from daylight till dark and on Sunday we'uns do us washin'. Church? Shucks, we'uns don't know what dat mean.

"I has de correct mem'randum [memory] of when de [civil] war start. Massa Black sold we'uns right den. Mammy and pappy powerful glad to git sold, and dey and I is put on de block with 'bout ten others . . . When we'uns git te de tradin' block, dere lots of white folks dere what come to look us over. One man shows de intres' in pappy. . . . He talk to pappy and pappy talk to him and say, 'Dem my woman and chiles. Please buy all of us and have mercy on we'uns.' "

Former plantation slave Rose Williams, interviewed as an elderly woman in 1941, had a brutal master. Although pleased to be put up for sale, her family feared separation.

most basic possessions. No "separate spheres" existed here—everyone lived and worked together.

WOMEN IN SLAVERY

The home life of enslaved women was even tougher. Masters could separate husbands from wives, and children from their parents, by selling family members. Many women were raped by their master and forced to bear his children. Since families were often divided, women formed the bedrock of the family—which usually consisted of a mother and her small children.

Within the enslaved community, women experienced less discrimination by gender than white women because all slaves lacked power. They

---

Below: An engraving of an African-American woman being separated from her child at a slave auction, around 1840.

1840.]   *Anti-Slavery Almanac.*   15

SELLING A MOTHER FROM HER CHILD.

" 'Do you *often* buy the wife without the husband?' 'Yes, *very often* ; and *frequently*, too, they sell me the mother while they keep her children. I have often known them take away the infant from its mother's breast, and keep it, while they sold her.' "—*Prof. Andrews, late of the University*

all did physical work, and none owned property. Black women had more freedom than white women in their personal lives. Since slave marriages were not legal, a couple could decide to live apart if the relationship broke down. Enslaved women had tiny homes and little time for housework, so the ideal of separate spheres simply did not apply.

MIGRATING TO THE WEST

In the early and mid-1800s, vast numbers were on the move from rural areas to cities or to the West. From the late 1840s, white people traveled to the recently acquired territories of New Mexico, Oregon, and California. They usually chose to migrate, but Native Americans were forced to move. Their communities were sent farther and farther west as whites settled their land.

Life in the West presented challenges for white women pioneers. In western towns, they had to interact with a mixture of people, often including Chinese, Mexicans, Native Americans, and immigrants from Europe. Many found it hard living in an isolated environment in basic housing with poor

Above: A wagon train hit by a snowstorm on the Great Plains. Travelers had little protection from extreme weather conditions.

WOMEN OF COURAGE AND CONVICTION

CLARA BROWN (c. 1803–85)

Some free black men and women migrated west. Born into slavery in Virginia, Clara Brown's family was twice broken up by slave auctions. She lived for twenty years in Kentucky, and was freed when her owner died in 1857. Liberated slaves had to leave Kentucky. Clara went to Leavenworth, Kansas; then in 1859 she joined a wagon train to walk 700 miles (1,130 km) to Colorado. She was one of only six women and the only African American making the exhausting and perilous journey. Upon arrival in Denver, Clara established her own laundry business. In 1866 she returned to Kentucky and helped sixteen former slaves to travel to Colorado to make a new life.

AN ABUNDANCE OF FOOD

"I have worked at a hotel for five weeks, doing washing and ironing; and I enjoy the best treatment, though I cannot speak with the people. I have food and drink in abundance. A breakfast here consists of chicken, mutton, beef, or pork, warm or cold wheat bread, butter, white cheese, eggs, or small pancakes, the best coffee, tea, cream, and sugar.
. . . My greatest regret here is to see the superabundance of food, much of which has to be thrown to the chickens and the swine, when I think of my dear ones in Bergen [in Norway], who like so many others at this time lack the necessaries of life."

Jannicke Saehle, a young single woman from Norway, wrote her brother in Norway to tell him about her job and the luxurious food available in America.

facilities. They discovered that the manners and morals of polite society in the East generally did not apply in the West.

However, women experienced benefits of the move west, too. They had more freedom, and the lack of females meant there was a huge demand for women as wives. The labor shortage allowed them to take advantage of new business opportunities. For instance, women who went to California during the gold rush could use their domestic skills to cook for people or run boardinghouses.

IMMIGRANTS TO THE WEST

Large numbers of immigrants, especially from Scandinavia, picked the West as their destination and moved to the Great Plains in the mid-19th century. In the 1840s, there was an increase in Norwegian immigration. Many were farmers who wanted land.

Below: The Cherokee people had to move west following the Indian Removal Act. Their forced departure from Georgia in 1838 became known as the Trail of Tears. It is estimated that about 15,000 of the 100,000 people who left Georgia died on the journey west.

NATIVE AMERICANS—FORCED TO MOVE

There was white migration to the Southeast too, which forced Native Americans to leave their land and resources and lose their independence. The Indian Removal Act (1830) gave the government the legal power to move them. The government and missionaries also tried to impose European gender relations on Native Americans. They encouraged Native American women to limit their work to the home and men to take control of land and property. This created tension between men and women. After the southeastern communities had resettled in the West, men gained ever-increasing political power in tribal government, although they did give women land and property rights.

Below: Mexicans dancing the *fandango* in California in the 19th century. While ruled by Mexico, women in the Southwest could keep control of their own property and had the right to sue people in court. Once the United States took over the region, American laws replaced the Mexican traditions.

TURNING POINT

INDIAN REMOVAL ACT, 1830

During the 1820s, land in the Southeast, east of the Mississippi River, was rapidly settled by Europeans. They were not prepared to share the land, even with peaceful Native Americans. The Indian Removal Act allowed the government to remove Native Americans from their territories in Florida, Georgia, Alabama, and Mississippi and send them to unsettled prairie land in the West. More than 45,000 people had to relocate; they mostly ended up in Oklahoma. Although the Native Americans forced to move were told their right to the new territory would be guaranteed, the westward expansion over the following decades often pushed them even farther west.

CHAPTER 3

WORKING LIFE

THE WORKING LIVES OF WOMEN VARIED ENORMOUSLY depending on their position in society and where they lived. The ideology of separate spheres limited most middle-class women to domestic work in the home. In the South, a small number of white women were members of slave-owning families. They supervised slaves, distributed food, oversaw the garden, cared for farm animals, and managed the household's production of goods. In contrast, working-class women of all races worked both in and outside the home to enable their families to survive.

Above: A farming woman undertakes the daily task of milking the cows. Women were also in charge of producing dairy products such as milk and cheese.

COUNTRY WOMEN

In rural areas, women worked to produce almost everything the family needed. They planted vegetables in their gardens, tended fruit orchards, drove cattle, milked cows, and raised chickens and hogs. They also made farm products and household goods to be sold in shops in towns, including butter, homespun cloth, and tallow for making candles.

According to southern ideals, women were frail and required protection; hard manual labor was deemed unsuitable. Farm work was seen as the job of slaves. Yet the wives and daughters of poor southern farmers often worked in the fields alongside men, planting, harvesting, and sowing crops.

TOWNSWOMEN

In towns, women were unable to produce their own food. To boost the family income so they could afford to buy food and other necessities, they did various jobs. They took in needlework or ran a grocery or tavern from home. Some accepted boarders, offering them food and a bed and doing their laundry. Women also worked as street vendors and washerwomen.

FREE AFRICAN-AMERICAN WOMEN

Free black women led even tougher lives. Segregated from white society, they generally existed in poverty. Many were single mothers, having been separated from their husbands by their former masters.

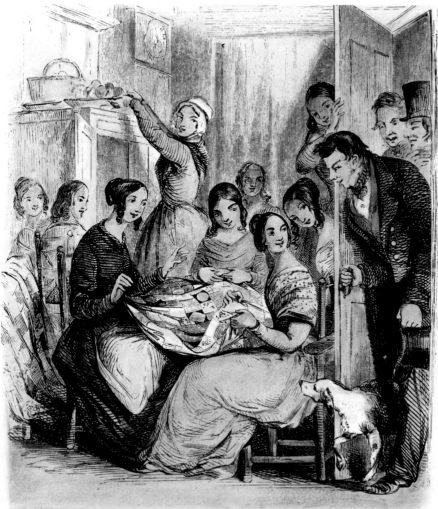

THE QUILTING PARTY.

FARMWORK

"[I have,] in fact, seen more white native American women at work in the hottest sunshine in a single month, and that near mid-summer, than in all my life in the free states. . . . Not on account of an emergency, as in harvesting, either, but in the regular cultivation of cotton and of corn [but] chiefly of cotton."

In his book *A Journey in the Back Country* (1861), Frederick Olmsted wrote about seeing white women hard at work in the fields.

Left: Women made quilts for bedding. By the early 1800s, cotton fabrics were being produced in factories, reducing the cost of quilt making.

A FULL DAY

"[I feel] very unwell, but with the assistance of my ever-dear C[harity], wash 5 flannel sheets, 5 flannel shimmies [women's undergarments], 1 waist [blouse], & 6 pairs of stockings, 13 towels, 3 table cloths, & 3 pair of pillow cases, 3 aprons, 1 night gown, 5 handkerchiefs, clean the buttery, cupboard, bedchamber, dining room & kitchen, make crackers & bake them."

Sylvia Drake and Charity Bryant ran a tailor (clothes-making) shop in Weybridge, Vermont, during the early 1800s. This entry from Sylvia's diary on April 27, 1822, indicates the heavy workload involved in making a living and running a household—and on this day Sylvia was ill.

"

A GOOD TIME

"Ever since I wuzza little bit'ah [young] gal I stayed rite in de house wid ma' Mistus [mistress], played wid de white chillun [children], slep' in deir [their] beds an' et' rite at deir table. In ma' case, I had just'ta good'ah time 'fore de Yanks [northern troops] came as I did a'ter de war. I waited on de' white chillun, set de table an' toted [brought] de food f'om de kitchen to de dinin' room."

As a child before the Civil War, Sarah Fitzpatrick was a house servant for a white family. Later, she talked about how she played with the white children but had to work for them, too.

They did the most menial jobs, for instance, working as servants, cooks, and laundresses. Even married free black women had to do paid work. Owing to discrimination, free black men were offered only the lowest-paid jobs, which tended to be irregular or seasonal. This meant that wives' labor was necessary to contribute to the household income. Like their white counterparts in the towns, many African-American women took in boarders.

BLACK WOMEN IN THE SOUTH

In the South, enslaved women worked just as hard as men, doing backbreaking physical labor on the region's cotton, tobacco, and sugarcane plantations. No task was deemed too arduous for a black woman. Those who worked as domestic servants in white households had a less strenuous working life but were tied to the continual service of their master's family. Even the small children of slaves were expected to work for their keep.

Below: Cotton being harvested in 1860 by enslaved women and men. A white overseer keeps a close eye on the workers. The invention of the cotton gin mechanized part of the cotton production process, but the crop still had to be harvested by hand.

Above: Women weaving at a textile mill in Lowell, Massachusetts, in the 1850s. Although the mill owners intended to provide good conditions, the work was dull and repetitive, and the factories were poorly lit and ventilated.

MEXICAN WOMEN AT WORK

Mexican women in the frontier areas—the Mexican states that became part of the United States in the 1840s—benefited from a certain amount of freedom. The region was underpopulated and there was a shortage of labor, so there were plenty of opportunities to work outside the home. Women could adopt various trades, for example, becoming bakers, weavers, or craftspeople. They also became farmers and ranchers.

NEW INDUSTRIES, NEW JOBS

The new industries of the mid-19th century offered some women (mostly white) the chance to earn wages, for example, in shoe factories and mills. It was in manufacturing that the female labor force was most noticeable. By 1850, women made up almost a quarter of the workforce.

In the 1820s and 1830s, huge textile mills were constructed in the Northeast. Factory towns sprang up, such as Waltham and Lowell, Massachusetts. The mill owners employed young single women from

TURNING POINT

THE LOWELL COMMUNITIES

At Lowell, the employers wanted a well-behaved and orderly labor force, working in decent conditions. In 1826, Francis Cabot Lowell's business partners formed the town of Lowell and built an industrial city. They set up company-owned boardinghouses for their young female employees, who were mostly from New England. These unique communities provided facilities and services that were intended to uplift the inhabitants, such as a library and religious instruction. The strict rules included attendance at church. Most mill girls worked for about four years and then returned home to marry or to find another job. The scheme attracted worldwide interest. The Lowell communities flourished from the 1820s through the 1840s.

"

LONG HOURS

"She complained of the hours for labor being too many, and the time for meals too limited. In the summer season, the work is commenced at 5 o'clock a.m., and continued till 7 o'clock, p.m., with half an hour for breakfast and three quarters of an hour for dinner. . . . The air in the room she considered not to be wholesome. . . . Thinks that there is no day when there are less than six of the females out of the mill from sickness. . . . She herself is out quite often, on account of sickness. . . .

"She thought there was a general desire among the females to work but ten hours, regardless of pay."

After receiving a petition, in 1845 the Massachusetts state legislature held public hearings on industrial working conditions for the first time in the United States. Weaver Eliza R. Hemmingway was the first to testify.

rural areas in their factories to work power looms. The women were already used to farm labor and producing goods from home. For their efforts, they were paid half the rate of skilled male workers. Even with years of experience, a woman factory worker earned less than her male co-workers. Yet the mills offered the highest wages available to working-class women; the pay was similar to that of a teacher. A job in the mills was therefore a good option.

LOWELL WOMEN STRIKE AND PROTEST

During the 1830s and 1840s, the mill owners became determined to increase their profits. They introduced speedups, forcing workers to work faster, and wage cuts. The conditions in the Lowell boardinghouses deteriorated. In 1834 and 1836 and also in the 1840s, hundreds of Lowell women workers went on strike in protest over the decline in conditions.

In 1844, Lowell mill workers formed the Lowell Female Labor Reform Association to try to improve their working conditions. Its president was Sarah Bagley. The Reform Association organized

Below: A view of Boott cotton mills in Lowell, Massachusetts, which began operation in the late 1830s. The young women workers were kept under strict supervision even on their days off and were subject to curfews.

a petition to reduce the workday to ten hours (most women worked eleven to thirteen hours daily). It was signed by people throughout the Lowell mill towns, and the Association presented it to the Massachusetts state legislature (lawmakers). A committee investigated conditions at Lowell in 1845 but rejected the demand. After 1845, the factory owners began to board workers individually to stop them from organizing together. From 1847, the Reform Association shifted its focus to assisting members facing difficulties.

IMMIGRANT FACTORY WORKERS

Another reason for the decline in the mill workers' protest movement was the mill owners' use of immigrant labor. During the 1840s, Irish and central European immigrants arrived in the United States in large numbers. As newcomers eager for employment, they were prepared to work for lower wages than native-born workers. They began to replace the white farm girls in the factories. During the 1850s, when companies imposed wage cuts and a decline in working conditions, most native-born female workers left the industry. By 1860, nearly a quarter of the mill workforce was made up of Irish women.

Below: Here German and Irish immigrants arrive in New York, around 1860. The immigrants had escaped desperate poverty in their own country and on arrival were eager to take on any kind of work available.

BREAKTHROUGH BIOGRAPHY

SARAH G. BAGLEY (1806–c. 1883)

Born in New Hampshire to a family who farmed and owned a small mill, Sarah Bagley went to work in a cotton mill in Lowell, Massachusetts, in 1836. Along with five other weavers, in 1844 Sarah founded the Lowell Female Labor Reform Association (FLRA). By 1845, she was working full time as an organizer, setting up FLRA branches in other towns. However, the legislature took no action on the demand for a ten-hour workday, and the campaign declined. After a year working as the first female telegraph operator in America, Sarah returned to mill work in 1848. In 1850, she married James Durno. The couple moved to New York the following year and set up a clinic offering natural remedies.

Right: Astronomer Maria Mitchell. By 1860, she had become the best-known woman scientist in the United States and went on to become a professor of astronomy and the director of an observatory—the first woman to hold either of these positions.

WOMEN OF COURAGE AND CONVICTION

ELIZABETH BLACKWELL (1821–1910)

Born in England, Elizabeth Blackwell moved to the United States in 1832. She was determined to be a doctor. Surprisingly for a woman, she succeeded in her application to Geneva Medical College, New York, in 1847. Yet many students and local townspeople thought it wrong for a woman to study medicine; she was frequently harassed or ignored. Elizabeth persevered and graduated first in her class in 1849. She undertook further medical training in Paris and London. Returning to New York in 1851, she was refused work in the city's hospitals because she was a woman. Eventually, in 1853, she established a clinic in a slum district, which in 1857 was greatly enlarged to form the New York Infirmary for Women and Children.

OPENING UP THE PROFESSIONS

Women were barred from the best-paid professions of law, medicine, and the military. Although they worked as midwives, caring for women in childbirth, they were not permitted to be physicians. It was thought that women were too delicate to cope with the gory dissection of bodies at medical school. The first medical school to train female doctors, the Female Medical College of Philadelphia, opened in 1850. However, no woman was admitted to law school until after the Civil War.

Science was another profession denied to women. A rare exception was Maria Mitchell. She started out helping her father, an amateur astronomer. In 1847, Maria discovered a new comet and became the first woman to have a successful career as a scientist. In 1850, she was elected to the American Association for the Advancement of Science—the only female member.

CHURCH MINISTERS

The Society of Friends (Quakers) and a few other small religious groups such as the Congregationalists employed female ministers. But most churches would not accept women preaching in public.

TEACHING

In contrast, by 1860, teaching was seen as a respectable job for single women. As female education expanded, so did the number of women teachers. Teachers did not have to train or achieve formal qualifications, and many young educated women taught school for a few years before getting married. Yet female teachers always received far less pay than men for doing the same job. Susan B. Anthony was outraged to discover that male teachers at her school in the 1840s earned $10 a week while women received just $2.50.

> ## BREAKTHROUGH BIOGRAPHY
>
> ### ANTOINETTE BROWN (1825–1921)
>
> Born in New York, Antoinette Brown joined the Congregational Church as a child. (Congregationalists hold that all individuals can come to God, without the need for priests. Each church is independent and employs its own minister.) After gaining a degree from Oberlin College in 1847, Antoinette enrolled in the theology program—unheard of for a woman. When she completed her studies in 1850, the college refused to grant her a degree. In 1853, she was ordained as a minister in the First Congregational Church in New York but left a year later to become a minister in the Unitarian Church. (This church believes in the unity of God rather than the Holy Trinity.) In addition to preaching, she was involved in the abolitionist, temperance, and women's rights movements. In 1856, Antoinette married Samuel Blackwell, brother of Elizabeth Blackwell, and they raised five daughters. In later years, she wrote several books about the physical and social sciences.

Left: An early 19th-century dame school. Since colonial times, women had run dame schools in their own homes, providing a basic education in reading, writing, and arithmetic for girls. As education for girls expanded, dame schools were replaced.

CHAPTER 4

WOMEN'S ORGANIZATIONS

WOMEN COULD NOT TAKE PART IN ELECTORAL POLITICS, but many middle-class women, mostly white, became involved in public life—especially in the Northeast and the Midwest. Large numbers joined religious and charitable societies. These associations did not challenge men's role since the women were keeping to their sphere. In fact, the ideology of separate spheres inspired them to act. Women were seen as responsible for maintaining the welfare and moral standards of their family. Helping their community was the next logical step.

RELIGIOUS, CHARITABLE, AND REFORM ORGANIZATIONS

The religious revival inspired the establishment of Bible societies, missionary societies, and Sunday schools. Women also established charitable organizations, for example, to fund schools for the poor and to assist widows, orphans, and disabled people.

Below: A Sunday school in the American West in the mid-19th century. The teachers taught the children hymns, told them Bible stories, and had them memorize Bible verses.

Above: A contemporary image of an institution for the mentally ill in New York, 1868. The inmates were not treated as human beings. Officials believed that "lunatics" could not feel the cold, so the buildings were not heated.

Religious zeal, along with a rise in social problems, sparked a social reform movement in the 1830s and 1840s. The huge changes brought about by industrialization, urbanization, and immigration caused the problems, but there were not enough institutions to deal with them. Women reformers, particularly in the Northeast, took up the challenge.

MENTAL HEALTH REFORM

Health was one area requiring reform. For example, in the early 19th century, people with mental health problems were usually locked up in jail or imprisoned in their family's home. Dorothea Dix, a remarkable reformer, dedicated herself to the improvement of the lives of the mentally ill.

The most popular movements promoted moral reform, such as the prevention of prostitution. Prostitution was on the rise; for instance, an 1832 survey indicated that there were 10,000

WOMEN OF COURAGE AND CONVICTION

DOROTHEA DIX
(1802–87)

In 1841, Dorothea Dix, a former teacher, was asked to teach Sunday school in a prison in East Cambridge, Massachusetts. She was appalled to find that mentally ill people were imprisoned alongside criminals, left naked in their cells, in darkness and without heating. Many of them were in chains. Dorothea traveled throughout the state and found similar conditions. Over the next forty years, she successfully lobbied for the reform of treatment for people with mental health problems in fifteen states. She personally oversaw the establishment of thirty-two mental hospitals.

PROSTITUTION

"L.C.G.: the examining officer reports in this case, 'This girl (a tailoress) is a stranger without any relations. She received a dollar and a half a week, which would not maintain her.' . . . E.M.G.: the captain of police in the district where this woman resides says, 'This girl struggled hard with the world before she became a prostitute, sleeping in station-houses at night, and living on bread and water during the day. . . . In my experience of three years, I have known over fifty cases whose history would be similar to hers, and who are now prostitutes.' "

In 1858, physician William Sanger presented his research on prostitution in New York. When he interviewed prostitutes, he found that the commonest reason for turning to prostitution was dire poverty.

DEMON DRINK

"Drunkenness is good ground for divorce, and every woman who is tied to a confirmed drunkard should sunder [break] the ties; and if she do it not otherwise the law should compel it—especially if she have children. . . . Can it be possible that the moral sense of a people is more shocked at the idea of a pure-minded, gentle woman sundering the ties which bind her to a loathsome mass of corruption, than it is to see her dragging out her days in misery, tied to his besotted and filthy carcass?"

The Woman's New York State Temperance Society adopted a resolution in 1852 stating that a woman should be able to divorce her husband if he was an alcoholic. Many people, especially in the press and the churches, were shocked by this viewpoint. In this speech, Amelia Bloomer backed the resolution.

prostitutes in New York City. Moral reform societies aimed to close brothels and save men from vice.

THE TEMPERANCE MOVEMENT

This campaign attracted more support than any other reform movement in the antebellum period. In the mid-19th century, heavy drinking was a feature of men's social lives. Factory workers drank beer during their lunch breaks and at social and political gatherings. Liquor affected family life. Some men spent a large proportion of their hard-earned wages on drinking. When they were drunk, men were more likely to be violent toward their wives and children. Women therefore had a great interest in the temperance movement.

THE WOMAN'S NEW YORK STATE TEMPERANCE SOCIETY

This society was set up in 1852 because existing temperance societies did not permit women to join. Its founding members included Elizabeth Cady Stanton, Susan B. Anthony, and Amelia Bloomer—

Below: Men drinking in a barroom in New Orleans, Louisiana, in 1848. Only men socialized in bars.

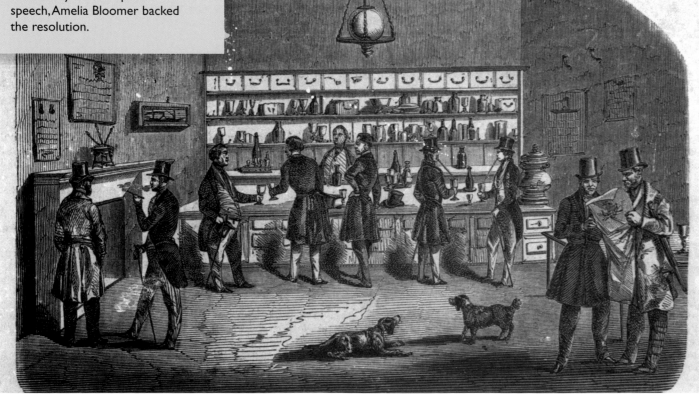

EARLY VICTORIES

The temperance movement achieved some results in the 1850s. In 1851, Maine became the first state to outlaw the production and sale of liquor, and twelve more states passed similar laws in the 1850s. The movement laid the foundations for the temperance campaign of the 1870s, which became a nationwide movement.

Left: A women's group protests against drunkenness and alcoholism by singing in front of a public house in 1874.

women who were also to become key activists in the struggle for women's rights. Members of the group petitioned, lectured, and put pressure on state and local governments to change the law to prevent the sale of liquor. Although it was unacceptable at the time for women to speak in public, members of the society traveled around New York State talking to female audiences about how drunkards caused problems for their families.

Despite their contribution to the campaign against drunkenness, the women's temperance societies were not fully accepted by the men's organizations. Many clergymen in the temperance movement opposed women's involvement, firmly believing they should stick to domestic and religious roles. Women were not allowed to take part in conventions (conferences). In 1853, for instance, representatives from the Woman's New York State Temperance Society were refused admission to a meeting of the World's Temperance Convention.

Many women realized it was hard to speak out in society when they suffered so much discrimination. After the 1850s, the temperance

Right: An 1847 image of a wedding by Nathaniel Currier. According to the principle of *feme covert*, a woman had no independent legal existence once she married.

TURNING POINT

THE MARRIED WOMEN'S PROPERTY ACT, 1848

Under the Married Women's Property Act, passed in New York, women who married could keep control of their property and the rents and profit they received from it—just as single women did. They could keep any property given to them while they were married, for example, if a family member left it to them in a will. The New York law became the model for similar acts introduced across the country over the following fifty years.

movement declined for a while, and many activists entered the struggle for women's rights in general.

FIGHTING FOR PROPERTY RIGHTS

The restrictions women faced led some determined individuals to fight to improve their rights, for example, over property. In the early 19th century, a woman gave up control of her property and wages when she married. This came from the English common law tradition, brought to America by settlers. On marriage, a woman became a *feme covert*, or "covered woman," which meant that her legal existence was incorporated into that of her husband. All her possessions belonged to him. If she earned any money, he took control of it. She also was not able to sign contracts or claim custody of her children in the rare circumstance of a divorce.

In 1836, Judge Thomas Hertell of the New York state legislature introduced a bill proposing that wives have the right to claim their property. Ernestine L. Rose worked to gain support for the bill and eventually helped to achieve the Married Women's Property Act of 1848. Although it did not achieve full legal rights for women, it was a step in the right direction.

During the 1850s, Rose and other female campaigners made the case for further reform to the New York state legislature. Eventually, in 1860, it passed an additional act giving greater rights to married women. They could maintain their property separate from their husband's and keep their own earnings. Yet they still required their husband's permission to sell their property.

PROPERTY RIGHTS AND SUFFRAGE

The issue of property rights gave rise to questions about the entitlement to suffrage. Many people felt that those with property had a stake in the country and should be allowed to vote. Some states had a property qualification for voting— people had to be homeowners to take part in elections. However, women and non-white men might own property but could not vote. Now that married women could keep their property, the argument that they should have suffrage was strengthened.

Right: Ernestine Rose, pictured in the 1850s. In 1840, she joined with Elizabeth Cady Stanton and Paulina Wright (later Wright Davis) to petition for married women's property rights.

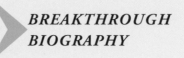

BREAKTHROUGH BIOGRAPHY

ERNESTINE L. ROSE (1810–92)

Born a Polish Jew, Ernestine Polowsky gave up her faith when young, and left Poland. She lived in several other European countries. In 1836, while in England, she married William E. Rose and they emigrated to the United States. Once there, Ernestine was dismayed at the lack of women's rights. During the 1840s, she lobbied in New York State to change the law that deprived married women of the right to keep property they had owned before marriage. Ernestine organized a petition drive every year, which helped to secure the passage of New York's Married Women's Property Act in 1848. In the 1850s, she was active in the newly formed women's rights movement as well as the temperance and abolitionist movements. She continued to fight for women's suffrage in the following decades.

" FASHION STATEMENT

"About this time [1851], Elizabeth Smith Miller . . . appeared on the streets of our village [Seneca Falls] dressed in short skirts and full Turkish trousers. . . . A few days after Mrs. Miller's arrival in Seneca Falls Mrs. Stanton came out in a dress made in Mrs. Miller's style. . . . Having had part in the discussion of the dress question, it seemed proper that I should practise as I preached . . . and so a few days later I, too, donned the new costume, and in the next issue of my paper announced that fact to my readers. . . . As soon as it became known that I was wearing the new dress, letters came pouring in upon me by hundreds from women all over the country making inquiries about the dress and asking for patterns showing how ready and anxious women were to throw off the burden of long, heavy skirts."

In her book, *Life and Writings of Amelia Bloomer* (1895), the author talks about how the bloomers fashion caught on.

Above: A woman in a promenade dress and shawl in the 1860s. Wealthy women regularly wore heavy, cumbersome garments like these and were thought abnormal if they dressed otherwise.

THE DRESS REFORM MOVEMENT

Fighting for legal rights was one side of the struggle. Women also sought to free their own bodies from fashionable clothing. Middle- and upper-class women in the 19th century wore a corset to make them look slim. Not only was it uncomfortable, but this stiff garment also squeezed the abdominal area and caused damage to internal organs. All women wore long, heavy skirts, and the weight strained their backs.

In 1851, Elizabeth Cady Stanton's cousin, Elizabeth Smith Miller, invented her own comfortable outfit. She adopted a short dress worn over pantaloons (baggy pants)—and no corset. Amelia Bloomer printed the pattern for the novel outfit in the *Lily*, her newspaper. Although she had not invented the combination, it became known as "bloomers." The women who wore bloomers inspired great hostility among both sexes. People thought that it was unladylike and that the pants made them look like men. However, the women who tried them out were relieved to be able to move freely and enjoyed the lightness of the garments.

ARRESTS

Although bloomers were comfortable and practical, by 1854 the leaders of the women's rights movement had given up on dress reform. They felt it distracted from more important issues, so they returned to wearing regular clothes. The few women who still wore bloomers were subject to ridicule and, occasionally, arrest for wearing "men's clothing."

Below: This English cartoon from 1852 shows women confidently wearing the bloomer outfit, although the illustrator makes fun of the clothing and the notion of female emancipation.

WOMEN OF COURAGE AND CONVICTION

AMELIA BLOOMER (1818–94)

Amelia Jenks, from New York, married Quaker newspaper editor Dexter C. Bloomer in 1840. She grew interested in current affairs and started to write newspaper articles. Amelia joined the temperance movement in the 1840s, and toward the end of the decade, she became interested in the women's rights movement. In 1849, she set up the *Lily*, a newspaper for women. When she publicized the bloomers fashion in the paper, it created quite a stir. By 1853, Amelia had become active in the women's movement. That year, she and other women's rights leaders became the first women to address public meetings in New York. Amelia sold the *Lily* in 1856 but continued to write and lecture in favor of women's rights.

CHAPTER 5

THE ABOLITIONIST MOVEMENT

Whlle MOST FEMALE CAMPAIGNERS WERE ACTIVE in religious, charitable, or reform organizations, from the 1830s a tiny minority joined the more radical abolitionist movement. This was based mainly in the Northeast and Midwest. When women encountered male resistance to their involvement, they formed their own groups, and female leaders emerged to direct the movement. Black and white women took part, although some tensions existed between them.

"

THE STRENGTH OF A WOMAN

"Look at me! Look at my arm! (and she bared her right arm to the shoulder, showing her tremendous muscular power). I have ploughed, and planted, and gathered into barns, and no man could heed me! And a'n't I a woman? I could work as much and eat as much as a man—when I could get it—and bear de lash a well! And a'n't I a woman? I have borne thirteen chilern, and seen'em mos' all sold off to slavery, and when I cried out with my mother's grief, none but Jesus heard me! And a'n't I a woman?"

This excerpt from Sojourner Truth's 1851 speech "A'n't I a Woman?" appeared in the newspapers in a southern dialect although she was raised in upstate New York. Here she explains that African-American women were not protected like white women and were expected to work as hard as any man.

Right: An illustration of Sojourner Truth from a photograph, 1864–99. Sojourner Truth publicized slaves' anger with their lot and dispelled the myth that they were well cared for.

WOMEN OF COURAGE AND CONVICTION

HARRIET TUBMAN (c. 1820–1913)

Harriet Tubman was born into slavery in Maryland and put to work in the fields as a child. In 1849, her master died. Fearful that they would be sold to slave owners in the Deep South, she and her brothers escaped to the North. They were assisted by the Underground Railroad, a network of volunteers who secretly helped slaves escape from the South. Harriet moved to Philadelphia, where she lived as a free woman. Determined to assist others like herself, she then made nineteen return trips to the South over the following ten years and rescued about three hundred enslaved people. Supporters of slavery considered her a serious threat. One time in 1860, she was attacked and beaten after helping a runaway slave to escape from the police in New York. During the Civil War, Harriet worked for the Union Army.

Left: Harriet Tubman, shown here, played a significant role in the abolitionist movement. It is worth noting that although the movement was an important part of United States history, it never became a mass campaign and probably attracted no more than 1 percent of the population.

AFRICAN-AMERICAN ABOLITIONISTS

During the 1830s, black women started to play an important role in abolitionism. In the North, they organized women's anti-slavery associations. The first such organization in the United States was founded by Mary A. Bathys in Salem, Massachusetts, in 1832. In the same year, Maria W. Stewart became the first African-American woman to speak out in public to audiences of men and women.

In general, black women found it difficult to make their voices heard in society. They suffered double discrimination, as women and as black people, and were disadvantaged by their lack of education. Only a few African-American women, including Sojourner Truth and Harriet

WOMEN OF COURAGE AND CONVICTION

LUCRETIA MOTT (1793–1880)

Lucretia Mott, a minister in the Society of Friends (Quakers), believed that slaves should be granted immediate freedom. She attended the founding convention of the American Anti-Slavery Society in 1833 and then set up the Philadelphia Female Anti-Slavery Society, becoming its president. In 1840, Lucretia was elected as an official delegate to the World Anti-Slavery Convention in London, but when she arrived, she discovered that women were not permitted to participate. Frustrated with the discrimination she experienced as a woman, from that time on Lucretia dedicated herself to the women's rights movement, writing articles and lecturing. She was a powerful speaker, standing her ground amid hostile audiences and arguing that God intended men and women to be equal.

Right: Lucretia Mott was a pioneer reformer who helped to establish the women's rights movement in the United States.

Tubman, achieved national recognition in the abolitionist movement. For instance, at the Second Women's Rights Convention in Akron, Ohio, in 1851, Sojourner Truth was determined to take the platform despite some opposition in the audience to a black woman speaker. Her remarkable speech had a powerful impact.

WHITE WOMEN OPPOSE SLAVERY

White northern women took part in setting up anti-slavery associations. They helped to found the New England Anti-Slavery Society in 1832 with abolitionist William Lloyd Garrison. However, in 1833, when the American Anti-Slavery Society was established in Philadelphia, women were not invited to participate. So they set up their own organizations. Lucretia Mott and others set up the biracial Philadelphia Female Anti-Slavery Society, and Maria Weston Chapman established the Boston Female Anti-Slavery Society, also open to both African-American and

FIFTH ANNIVERSARY
OF THE
MASSACHUSETTS ANTI-SLAVERY SOCIETY,
WEDNESDAY, JANUARY 25, 1837.

[☞ The public meetings, during the day, will be held in the SPACIOUS LOFT, OVER THE STABLE OF THE MARLBOROUGH HOTEL, and in the evening, in the REPRESENTATIVES' HALL.]

HOURS OF THE MEETINGS.

Meeting for Delegates at 9 o'clock in the morning, at 46, Washington-Street.

First public meeting at 10 o'clock A. M., in the LOFT OVER THE STABLE OF THE MARLBOROUGH HOTEL.

Second public meeting at 1-2 past 2 o'clock, P. M. same place.

Evening meeting at 1-2 past 6 o'clock, in the REPRESENTATIVES' HALL.

☞ The Committee of Arrangements respectfully inform the ladies that ample accommodations have been prepared for them. The loft is spacious, clean, well warmed, and will accommodate, with ease and perfect safety, at least 1000 persons.

☞ AMOS DRESSER, a citizen of this State, who was 'Lynched' at Nashville, for the crime of being an Abolitionist, will be present, and during the meetings in the afternoon and evening, will give a history of that affair.

By virtue of special compact, Shylock demanded a pound of flesh, cut nearest to the heart. Those who sell mothers separately from their children, likewise claim a legal right to human flesh; and they too cut it nearest to the *heart.—L. M. Child.*

On. woman! from thy happy hearth
Extend thy gentle hand to save
The poor and perishing of earth—
The chained and stricken slave!
Oh, plead for all the suffering of thy kind—
For the crushed body and the darkened mind. *J. G. Whittier.*

Above: This public meeting notice is worded specifically to encourage women to attend.

European women. Many others followed, and by 1837 there were female anti-slavery societies in twelve states.

While not personally affected by slavery like their African-American counterparts, white abolitionists fervently believed that slavery was a sin against God's will. They tried to persuade fellow Americans and the federal government to end this evil system. Their day-to-day activities included gathering signatures on petitions to Congress to outlaw slavery. They traveled around the country lecturing in favor of abolition.

THE GRIMKÉ SISTERS
Angelina and Sarah Grimké were hugely influential in the abolitionist movement. The sisters joined the Philadelphia Female Anti-Slavery Society in 1835. The following year, the American Anti-Slavery Society asked them to lecture

> **BREAKTHROUGH BIOGRAPHY**

ANGELINA GRIMKÉ (1805–79)
Angelina Grimké was born in South Carolina to a slaveholding family. Unusually for southern women, she and her sister Sarah strongly opposed slavery. They both became Quakers and moved to the North in 1829. Angelina joined the anti-slavery movement and was one of the first female abolitionists to speak out in public. In 1836, she published *Appeal to the Christian Women of the South.* In the book, she urged southern women to pay their slaves wages and to agitate against slavery. Angelina presented an anti-slavery petition to the Massachusetts state legislature in 1838, becoming the first woman to speak before a legislative body. That year, she married abolitionist Theodore Weld, who refused to accept the legal right to own his wife's property. After co-writing a book about slavery, Angelina's political activity declined. She was occupied bringing up her three children.

Above: Participants at the Fugitive Slave Law Convention in Cazenovia, New York, in 1850. They gathered to protest against the proposed fugitive slave law that would require law officers in states where slavery was illegal to arrest and return all escaped slaves. The law was passed despite opposition from abolitionists.

SISTERS IN BONDS

"We believe God gave woman a heart to feel—an eye to weep—a hand to work—a tongue to speak. Now let her use that tongue to speak on slavery. Is it not a curse—a heaven-daring abomination [vile practice]? Let her employ that hand, to labor for the slave. Does not her sister in bonds, labor night and day without reward? Let her heart grieve, and her eye fill with tears, in view of a female's body dishonored—a female's mind debased—a female's soul forever ruined! Woman [have] nothing to do with slavery!"

The Andover Female Anti-Slavery Society wrote this letter to the abolitionist newspaper the *Liberator* in 1836, calling for women to join the fight against slavery.

to female audiences in New York and New Jersey. Their talks were exceedingly popular, and soon they were speaking in packed churches and meeting halls to audiences of both sexes.

THE ANTI-SLAVERY CONVENTION OF AMERICAN WOMEN

The confidence of the women in the abolitionist movement increased. In 1837, an inter-racial meeting was held in New York City—the Anti-Slavery Convention of American Women. Wider society was shocked at this conference of black and white women expressing political feelings together. The women pledged to collect one million signatures on a petition for abolition, and Angelina Grimké introduced a resolution that they should work harder to achieve their goal.

OPPOSITION TO WOMEN ABOLITIONISTS

The Grimkés were asked to lecture in New England in 1837, where they denounced the South and also the North's failure to oppose slavery. This upset New England's ministers doubly—women were speaking out in public to mixed audiences and encouraging other women to take up anti-slavery activities. The ministers responded by accusing the Grimkés of threatening the "female character" through their activities. Most people in America at the time agreed. They did not accept the Grimkés' assertiveness or the fact that they lectured in public.

Abolitionists were sometimes physically attacked for expressing their views. In 1838, at the second Anti-Slavery Convention of American Women in Philadelphia, pro-slavery protesters attacked the women attending the convention and set fire to Pennsylvania Hall, where the meeting was held. Lucretia Mott courageously helped women to escape from the burning building.

THE ABOLITIONIST MOVEMENT SPLITS

By 1839, women's strong commitment to the cause finally persuaded the American Anti-Slavery Society to accept them as full members, able to hold office and lecture. Not everyone in the movement agreed with this move. When in 1840 Abby Kelley Foster was elected to the organization's business committee, two ministers on the committee

♥ WOMEN OF COURAGE AND CONVICTION

ABBY KELLEY FOSTER (1810–87)

Abby Kelley Foster was brought up a Quaker and became a teacher. William Lloyd Garrison recruited her to the abolitionist movement in the 1830s, and from 1835 to 1837, she acted as secretary of the Lynn Female Anti-Slavery Society. Abby participated in the national women's anti-slavery conventions in 1837 and 1838. At the latter, she made a speech to a mixed audience of men and women. She was so successful that she was asked to become a full-time speaker and she gave up her teaching job. For assuming this public role, she was severely criticized by churchmen. Following her appointment to the business committee of the American Anti-Slavery Committee in 1840, she continued to travel constantly to lecture. It was an exhausting lifestyle. After marrying Stephen S. Foster in 1845, the couple lectured together until 1861.

Left: Lucretia Mott (center) and other abolitionists find themselves under violent attack by pro-slavery protesters for trying to hold a meeting, around the late 1830s.

A CHRISTIAN ARGUES FOR SLAVERY

"Slavery, even in his own land, is his destiny and his refuge from extinction [being wiped out]. Beautifully has the system begun to expand itself among us. Shorn of the barbarities with which a slavery established by conquest and maintained by brute force is always accompanied, we have begun to mingle with it the graces and amenities of the highest Christian civilization."

In the 1850s, southerner Louisa S. Cheves McCord, who had managed her own plantation, wrote many articles defending slavery. In this 1853 article, she attacked abolitionist Harriet Beecher Stowe and claimed that the Christian values of slave owners were helping to "civilize" black people.

resigned to protest her nomination. Several members, including Henry Stanton, left the organization and set up another group, the American and Foreign Anti-Slavery Society. The issue of women's rights had divided the abolitionist movement.

The abolitionist movement was split from within and also had to contend with strong opposition from slave owners. They argued that slavery was a humane institution and that they valued and cared for their slaves.

DOCUMENTING THE CRUELTY

Abolitionists undertook research and compiled evidence to refute the pro-slavery argument that slave owners had an economic interest in their slaves and therefore treated them well. In 1839, abolitionist Theodore Weld, with the help of the Grimké sisters, published *American Slavery as It Is*. The book clearly illustrated the brutality of the institution.

LINKING SLAVES' AND WOMEN'S RIGHTS

Regardless of their commitment to the abolitionist cause, women activists continually came up against discrimination as females. In 1840, Lucretia Mott was elected as delegate to the World Anti-Slavery Convention in London. Only after making the lengthy journey did

Right: This woodcut of a 19th-century illustration gives an idyllic image of a domestic slave caring for a planter's child. Strong relationships often did form between female slaves and their charges, but the long hours spent looking after the master's children severely limited the time they could spend with their own family.

she discover that the British organization would not allow women to attend. She argued forcefully for women's participation; eventually they were permitted to be present but were forbidden to sit with men or join in fully. Mott and Elizabeth Cady Stanton became friends at the convention and were determined to work together for women's rights and against slavery.

NORTH–SOUTH DIVIDE

During the 1850s, tensions between the North and the South rose dramatically over the extension of slavery to the western territories. Most people in the North did not want slavery to be extended but accepted its existence in the South. Yet the abolitionist movement demanded an immediate end to slavery everywhere. The movement gathered pace as the friction between North and South mounted, eventually leading to the Civil War (1861–65). Through their involvement as abolitionists, women learned to organize. The resistance they encountered from men when they campaigned against slavery reinforced in their minds the need to fight for women's rights too.

Below: An illustration made from an eyewitness account of the brutal whipping of a slave on a Virginia plantation.

FLOGGINGS

"This lady used to keep cowhides, or small paddles (called 'pancake sticks') in four different apartments in her house; so that when she wished to punish, or to have punished, any of her slaves, she might not have the trouble of sending for an instrument of torture. For many years, one or other, and often more of her slaves, were flogged every day; particularly the young slaves about the house, whose faces were slapped, or their hands beat with the 'pancake stick,' for every trifling offense—and often for no fault at all."

Angelina Grimké Weld gave her own eyewitness account of slavery to Theodore Weld, in 1839. Here she recounts the cruelty of a slave-owning woman who professed to be a good Christian but beat her slaves.

CHAPTER 6

CLAIMING THE VOTE

THE ABOLITIONIST MOVEMENT HAD A GREAT IMPACT on the suffrage movement. As women fought for slaves' human rights, they realized that they themselves suffered injustices. They began to argue that women should have equal rights with men, including the right to vote. At the time, the demand for women's rights appeared even more radical than the struggle to end slavery. Few men or indeed women agreed with the idea of female suffrage. Yet the movement to claim the vote laid the ground for reform in the future.

EQUAL IN GOD'S EYES

"I follow him [God] through all his precepts [principles], and find him giving the same directions to women as to men, never even referring to the distinction now so strenuously insisted upon between masculine and feminine virtues: this is one of the anti-christian [sic] 'traditions of men' which are taught instead of the 'commandments of God.' Men and women were CREATED EQUAL; they are both moral and accountable beings, and whatever is right for man to do, is right for woman."

Sarah Grimké's "Letters on the Equality of the Sexes and the Condition of Woman" was published as a pamphlet in 1838. She based her arguments for the equality of men and women on the Bible. Here she claims that God created them equal; it is male church leaders who teach that they are not.

THE GRIMKÉ SISTERS SPEAK OUT

Angelina and Sarah Grimké, outspoken opponents of slavery, argued that women should have the same rights as men and had the responsibility to act independently and voice their opinions in public.

Below: The presidential elections of 1844. At this time, the world of politics was considered a male sphere. Polling was held in places frequented by men, such as saloons and public halls.

42

This stand met with vigorous opposition. Most people believed that the Bible said women should not speak in public. In any case, the Grimké sisters became exhausted from lecturing and from the controversy they caused. By 1838, they had withdrawn from public speaking but continued to write and publish essays on women's rights.

THE 1840S

During this decade, the idea of women's rights gained more attention. Influential journalist Margaret Fuller criticized separate spheres, which limited women's opportunities. Some men started to champion women's rights. Unitarian minister Samuel J. May became the first mainstream church minister to support women's suffrage. As women's commitment to public life grew through their involvement in movements such as the temperance

WOMEN OF COURAGE AND CONVICTION

MARGARET FULLER (1810–50)

Born in Cambridge, Massachusetts, and educated at home, Margaret Fuller worked first as a teacher. In 1839, she started to earn her living running intellectual seminars for women in her home. After publishing a book in 1844, she was offered a job as a literary critic for the *New York Tribune*, becoming the first female in the United States to work as a professional journalist. In her next book, *Woman in the Nineteenth Century* (1845), she argued for equality between men and women. In 1846, Margaret became foreign correspondent for the *Tribune* and traveled to Europe. Living in Italy in 1847, she became caught up in the revolutionary movement that led to an uprising in 1848. She also secretly married an Italian nobleman (man of high social rank) and they had a child. In 1850, as the family sailed to the United States, the ship sank and, tragically, all aboard drowned.

Left: Margaret Fuller, the first female foreign correspondent and professional literary critic, in a daguerreotype (early form of photo) from 1846.

TURNING POINT

DECLARATION OF RIGHTS AND SENTIMENTS, 1848

At the Seneca Falls Convention, the Declaration of Rights and Sentiments was adopted. Modeled on the Declaration of Independence (1776), it stated the grievances and goals of the women's movement. The Declaration of Independence had proclaimed that "all men are created equal;" this declaration amended it to "all men and women are created equal." It finished with twelve resolutions, including the right to equal education, to enter into the professions, and to speak in public. The final demand for women's suffrage proved the most controversial. All the resolutions passed easily except this one, which was only narrowly accepted.

Although radical for its time, the declaration reflected the concerns of the mainly middle-class white women at the convention. For instance, it claimed that it was unjust to offer the vote to male immigrants, free black men, and males in poverty while denying it to white women, who were more deserving. Overall, though, the document represented a giant step for the women's movement.

movement and the fight for married women's property rights, they challenged the view that women should remain quietly in the home.

THE SENECA FALLS CONVENTION, 1848

In July 1848, Lucretia Mott and Elizabeth Cady Stanton organized the two-day Seneca Falls Convention on women's rights in Seneca Falls, New York. It was a momentous event. For the first time, around three hundred people, mostly women, gathered to discuss the injustices they felt as women and asserted that they were equal to men. Women vowed to take action to achieve their rights.

THE ROCHESTER CONVENTION

Two weeks after the Seneca Falls Convention, a larger meeting was held in Rochester, New York. For the first time, the meeting was chaired by a woman, Abigail Bush. Another novel

Below: This cartoon of the Seneca Falls Convention represents a feminist speaker denouncing men. The birth of the women's rights movement met with derision and hostility from most of the media.

"
RIGHT FOR BOTH

"We . . . express our conviction [strong belief] that all political rights which it is expedient [practical] for man to exercise, it is equally so for woman. All that distinguishes man as an intelligent and accountable being, is equally true of woman; and if that government only is just which governs by the free consent of the governed, there can be no reason in the world for denying to woman the exercise of the elective franchise [the vote], or a hand in making and administering the laws of the land. Our doctrine is that 'right is of no sex.' We therefore bid the women engaged in this movement our humble Godspeed [wish for success]."

Frederick Douglass wrote an article in the *North Star*, July 28, 1848, to demonstrate his support for equal rights for women.

practice was introduced: instead of allowing only invited speakers to address the audience, the debate was opened up for all to contribute. Women activists judged both the conventions to be a success.

The public reaction was different. Most of the media were scornful of the women's conventions, ridiculing the women as "sour old maids"—an insulting expression for unmarried women. A few gave their support, such as the *North Star*, which was published by Frederick Douglass. An African-American leader who fought for equality for both slaves and women, he linked the two causes as part of one struggle for human freedom. He had attended the Seneca Falls Convention and supported women's suffrage. Yet many abolitionists did not support equality for women because they were concerned that backing women could lose them support for abolition.

Right: A portrait of Elizabeth Cady Stanton holding her second daughter, Harriot, in 1856. Living in Seneca Falls with responsibility for her family, she was overwhelmed with domestic and child-care duties yet became determined to struggle for women's rights.

WOMEN OF COURAGE AND CONVICTION

ELIZABETH CADY STANTON (1815–1902)

Elizabeth's activist career began in the abolitionist movement. She married lawyer and abolitionist Henry Stanton in 1840. As a wife and mother of seven children, frustration with a woman's lot encouraged Elizabeth to become involved in organizing the Seneca Falls Convention in 1848. She was convinced that achieving the vote was essential for women to obtain other rights. While continuing with her domestic duties, Elizabeth became a mainstay of the new women's rights movement. In 1851, she befriended Susan B. Anthony, and they started working together. Elizabeth was a formidable speaker and writer, producing impressive articles, essays, and pamphlets to promote women's rights. She remained an activist all her life.

THE WOMEN'S RIGHTS MOVEMENT BEGINS

The Seneca Falls Convention marked the start of the women's rights movement. A big debate over the issue developed within society. Since religion was extremely important in people's lives, arguments over women's role were often discussed in religious terms. Leaders of the movement such as Lucretia Mott, Elizabeth Cady Stanton, and Lucy Stone challenged interpretations of the Bible that led to the conclusion that women were inferior.

THE 1850S

Throughout the decade, the women's movement held many conventions around the country to inform people and discuss how to change the laws. Since there was no formal organization, a national meeting was held every year (except 1857) to discuss how to further the cause. These were lively occasions. Opponents attended, as well as supporters, to debate with the speakers and heckle loudly.

The first national women's rights convention was in Worcester, Massachusetts, in 1850. It adopted various resolutions, including the demand for women's suffrage and equality for all before the law, including enslaved women. Sojourner Truth spoke at the convention, and Lucy Stone joined the movement there.

LECTURES AND PETITIONS

The movement grew during the 1850s. Activists lectured, petitioned, raised money, and wrote letters to the press. Lectures were particularly important. Listening to speakers was a popular

> ### BREAKTHROUGH BIOGRAPHY
>
> **LUCY STONE (1818–93)**
>
> Born near West Brookfield, Massachusetts, to a family with seven surviving children, Lucy saw from a young age how hard her mother had to work. Determined to have an education, she worked as a teacher to save money so she could attend Oberlin College. After graduating in 1847, she became a professional lecturer for the Massachusetts Anti-Slavery Society and for the women's rights movement. During the 1850s, Lucy was the best-known female lecturer in the United States. It was a stressful job owing to the extensive traveling and the strong opposition to the cause that she encountered. In 1854, she married Henry Blackwell but kept her surname in protest at the discrimination against married women. In 1858, she refused to pay tax on her property because she had no voice in the town government. In response, her family's household goods were seized. Lucy pursued the struggle for women's rights for the rest of her life.
>
> ---
>
> *Left:* Lucy Stone was a leading advocate for women's rights. She was particularly well known for her impressive public-speaking skills.

BREAKTHROUGH
BIOGRAPHY

SOJOURNER TRUTH
(c. 1797–1883)

Born into slavery, Sojourner was freed in 1827 and moved to New York City with her two youngest children in 1829. After experiencing a series of religious visions, in 1843 she left New York City. Adopting the name Sojourner Truth, she traveled around the country preaching the message of God's goodness. In 1846, she adopted the abolitionist cause and began to speak for the movement. In 1850, she published her autobiography, *A Narrative of Sojourner Truth*, to help gain sympathy for abolition, and she lectured throughout the Midwest. During the early 1850s, she was drawn to the women's suffrage cause and toured around the country arguing for equality regardless of race or gender.

form of entertainment in the mid-19th century and an excellent way of spreading ideas. Petition drives became a major form of political pressure. Occasionally, women carried out civil disobedience, for example, refusing to pay taxes because they had no vote.

PUBLICITY FOR THE MOVEMENT

To build the movement, media coverage was essential. Activists made good use of the press, regularly sending letters to sympathetic newspapers such as the *Liberator*, the *Frederick Douglass Paper* (formerly the *North Star*), and the *New York Tribune*. The women's papers—the *Lily* and the *Una*—provided a good outlet too. Sojourner Truth wrote an autobiography in 1850 and made a speech in 1851 that was widely reported in the media.

OPPOSITION TO WOMEN'S RIGHTS

People who opposed the expansion of women's rights made their views known too. Opposition came particularly from church ministers. Most felt that if women had the vote, they might have different opinions from the men of the family and bring disharmony to the household. Minister John Weiss of Bedford, Massachusetts, wrote in 1854 that ambitions for a public role would destroy a

Below: This 1868 cartoon is disparaging about the women's movement. It implies that if women had equal rights, they would neglect their domestic duties, leaving men to do the sewing and child care.

HOW IT WOULD BE, IF SOME LADIES HAD THEIR OWN WAY.

woman's femininity. It was wrong for a woman to preach in church, lecture to an audience, or seek a job in politics.

Arguments against women's rights were especially vehement in the South. Few southern women were interested in the movement. Plantation owner Louisa Cheves McCord (who was also pro-slavery) attacked the movement in her writings.

PROGRESS BY 1860

Although there was still great opposition in 1860, the issues of female suffrage and women's rights in general had been raised in society. A network of women activists existed, mostly in the Northeast. They sometimes felt disheartened by the apathy of most women in society. The women in the movement tended to be upper or middle class and educated. Their message did not resonate with most women, who were busy working all day, every day. Female workers sometimes went on strike to defend their conditions, but the heavy demands of daily life meant they had little time or energy to take up wider issues. The suffrage campaign had a long way to go.

Above: In 1860, thousands of shoemakers in Lynn, Massachusetts, went on strike because their wages had been slashed. Women played a vital role in the strike. In this engraving, they are marching behind the Lynn City Guards.

> ## LET US BE STRONG
>
> "Oh! Let us be the woman of God's make;
> No Mrs. Bloomer, Abby Kelley thing
> Aping man's vices, while our weaker frame
> knows not his harsher virtues.
> Let us be
> Strong—but as Woman; resolute in right—
> All woman—perfect woman."
>
> In this poem, Louisa Cheves McCord denounces the campaigners for women's rights, who she believed degraded all women. She thought women should stick to their sphere.

CHAPTER 7

EDUCATION AND THE MEDIA

I N THE EARLY 19TH CENTURY, MOST GIRLS HAD LITTLE EDUCATION; they had to help at home to support their families. Enslaved people had no right to education at all. By the 1820s, once the northern states had outlawed slavery, African Americans were permitted to go to school, but their access to education was limited. Then, between the 1820s and the Civil War, there was a huge increase in the building of schools and colleges—both for boys and girls.

"

STUDYING AT TROY

"Mrs. Willard's Seminary at Troy was the fashionable school in my girlhood, and in the winter of 1830, with upward of a hundred other girls, I found myself an active participant in all the joys and sorrows of that institution. . . . I had already studied everything that was taught there except French, music, and dancing, so I devoted myself to these accomplishments. As I had a good voice I enjoyed singing, with a guitar accompaniment, and, having a good ear for time, I appreciated the harmony in music and motion and took great delight in dancing. The large house, the society of so many girls, the walks about the city, the novelty of everything made the new life more enjoyable than I had anticipated."

Elizabeth Cady Stanton describes her experience of attending Troy Female Seminary in *Eighty Years and More (1815–1897): Reminiscences of Elizabeth Cady Stanton.*

Above: A classroom at a girls' school in about 1850. By the mid-19th century, there was a large increase in middle- and upper-class girls going to school and a dramatic rise in female literacy.

GIRLS' SCHOOLS

By the 1820s, the idea that educated women would be better at raising children had become popular. Female education was expanded, with dramatic results during the 1830s and 1840s. There was some state support. For example, in 1838 Pennsylvania lawmakers gave funds to set up female academies throughout the state. Churches, communities, and individuals gave money to set up girls' schools. The Methodist Church was especially active in promoting female education, while the Catholic Church built academies in Louisiana, Kentucky, and Maryland.

ACADEMIES AND SEMINARIES

Common schools for young children were usually coed, but it was believed that older boys and girls should be educated separately. Girls were taught in female academies and seminaries. In the early 19th century, the number of academies grew rapidly, both in the North and South. Usually boarding schools, they offered elementary and secondary education. The curriculum included English, modern languages, science, and mathematics. Seminaries were private schools for girls. Most focused on teaching domestic skills such as cooking and cleaning, but from the 1820s, a few new seminaries such as Troy and Holyoke offered academic subjects too. Many seminary girls later became missionaries or teachers.

AN EXTENSION OF THE HOME

Another enthusiastic individual who furthered the expansion of female education was Catharine Beecher, who founded two seminaries, including the Western Female Institute in Cincinnati, Ohio. Yet Catharine believed that women's role was in the home and that girls should study domestic subjects

WOMEN OF COURAGE AND CONVICTION

EMMA WILLARD (1787–1870)

Emma Willard was an imaginative educator. In 1821, she opened the Troy Female Seminary in New York, which became one of the leading schools in the country. Emma expanded the scope of female seminary education to include subjects traditionally studied only by boys, such as science, mathematics, and philosophy. She linked subjects such as history and geography so that students could understand the process of change instead of simply memorizing facts. Rather than disciplining students by beating them, as was common at the time, she talked to them about why they had misbehaved. Emma headed her seminary until 1838, when she left to embark on a career lecturing and writing about the need to improve female education.

Below: During the 1840s, Emma Willard (pictured here) traveled thousands of miles to take her message across America. In later life, she wrote science, history, and geography schoolbooks.

JOHN SARTAIN. Sc

> **BREAKTHROUGH BIOGRAPHY**

CATHARINE BEECHER (1800–78)

Catharine Beecher was school educated but also taught herself Latin, philosophy, Greek, mathematics, and the sciences. In 1823, she and her sister Mary founded a girls' school in Hartford, Connecticut, that became the Hartford Female Seminary in 1827. In 1832, Catharine opened the Western Female Institute in Cincinnati, but it closed five years later owing to financial problems. She then devoted herself to establishing schools and colleges in the Midwest and encouraging women to become teachers. She also focused on spreading her ideas in print. In the firm belief that homemakers needed training, in 1841 she published *A Treatise on Domestic Economy*. It provided detailed advice on every aspect of domestic life, including cooking, health, and child care. It proved hugely influential. Catharine's efforts contributed to the spread of education as Europeans moved to the western territories and helped lead to the introduction of domestic science in the school curriculum.

Right: A portrait of Catharine Beecher from about the 1850s. Although she encouraged women to seek an education and become teachers, Beecher disagreed with them becoming involved in political affairs such as the anti-slavery movement.

only, such as cooking, child care, and family health. For her, teaching was an extension of the caring role. In her book *The Duty of American Women to Their Country* (1845), she urged women to become teachers.

EDUCATION IN THE WEST

Catharine Beecher sent teachers to set up schools in pioneer communities in the West. These committed individuals did their best under difficult circumstances. Teachers described the shortage of proper schoolrooms and supplies, the makeshift housing conditions, the cold winters, and the lack of interest in religious practice.

HIGHER EDUCATION FOR WOMEN

Around the United States, the widening of horizons afforded by the new schools led women to demand access to higher education. Mount Holyoke Seminary, known as America's first women's college, was

Above: Mount Holyoke College was founded by chemist and educator Mary Lyon, who inspired students with her motto "Go where no one else will go, do what no one else will do." The seminary (renamed Mount Holyoke College from 1893) offered high-quality teaching.

founded in South Hadley, Massachusetts, in 1837. Courses included English grammar, geography, history, algebra, and science; students also carried out domestic tasks. Many Holyoke graduates became teachers, and many other women's colleges were patterned on the Holyoke model.

COED INSTITUTIONS

Extremely few higher education institutions opened as coed before the Civil War. Oberlin was the first college to accept female students alongside men, in 1837. This was positive, although male and female students were treated differently. For instance, it was prohibited for women to speak in public. As a

"

RAGGED AND DIRTY

"My school embraces both sexes, and all ages from five to seventeen, and not one can read intelligibly [clearly]. They have no idea of the proprieties [rules of behavior] of the schoolroom, or of study, and I am often at a loss to know what to do for them. Could you see them, your sympathies would be awakened, for there are few but what are ragged and dirty in the extreme. . . . I had to wait for two weeks before I could get three broken [window] panes mended, and a few poor benches brought in. My furniture now consists of these benches, a single board put up against the side of the room for a writing-desk, a few bricks for andirons [metal stands for supporting burning wood in a fireplace], and a stick of wood for shovel and tongs."

In this letter of 1847, a teacher in the West talks about the poverty there and the challenges of delivering education to the students.

> ## BREAKTHROUGH BIOGRAPHY

HARRIET BEECHER STOWE (1811–96)

The sister of Catharine Beecher, Harriet attended a girls' school and then Catharine's seminary in Hartford. She moved to Cincinnati, Ohio, with her sister and father in 1832 and taught at the Western Female Institute, also founded by Catharine. Harriet marred Calvin Ellis Stowe in 1836, and they had seven children. A talented writer, Harriet wrote a collection of stories, *The Mayflower*, published in 1843. She is best known for writing *Uncle Tom's Cabin* (1852), a detailed tale about slavery. Harriet had learned about life in the South from friends and visited herself; she had also met runaway slaves. Widely promoted by abolitionists, 350,000 copies of the book were sold within a year. In the South, it met with enormous disapproval. Harriet wrote two other books on the anti-slavery theme and continued to write novels in later life.

student, Lucy Stone complained that she was not permitted to read out her prize-winning essay.

LITERATURE AND THE MEDIA

Since girls' opportunities for education were still limited, the media was hugely important for female literacy. Girls and women educated themselves through reading and writing at home. Owing to the improvement in printing

Below: This picture sheet depicts the characters from *Uncle Tom's Cabin* for use in a paper-doll theater. The book was dramatized as a play, which proved hugely popular. Pro-slavery opponents claimed that details in the book were incorrect, so in 1853 Harriet published *A Key to Uncle Tom's Cabin*, with documents that supported her work.

technology and the distribution of newspapers, people no longer had to depend on local sources of information. Even if their lives were based around the home, women could order newspapers and magazines to be delivered so they could keep abreast of events.

NOVELS

During the 1820s, domestic novels appeared—books about home life and family, aimed at women. The first was Catharine Sedgwick's *New-England Tale* (1822). The novels presented female heroines whose goal was a happy home but who were prepared to take risks and work hard to succeed. Such books achieved great popularity during the 1850s and 1860s.

MAGAZINES

Most women's magazines also reinforced the view of women as homemakers. *Godey's Lady's Book*, established by Louis A. Godey in 1831, was a highly influential women's magazine. Although it supported female education and the acceptance of women nurses

WOMAN'S NATURE

"*What a wonderful change in public opinion concerning the powers of the female mind has been effected since our journal was first published! Then—that is, twenty years ago—very little interest was taken in female education. The subject of 'woman's rights' had been foolishly and clamorously [noisily] urged by a fear, who [which], with a 'zeal without knowledge' or discretion [judgment], would have broken down the barriers of true modesty, and destroyed the retiring graces of woman's nature.*"

In the editorial from January 1850, *Godey's Lady's Book* prides itself on its campaign for better education for females while maintaining separate spheres for men and women to preserve women's "modesty." It expresses opposition to the women's rights movement.

Below: An engraving from *Godey's Lady's Book* showing beautifully dressed women by the ocean. Fashion was an important element in the magazine.

and physicians, it encouraged women to follow a traditional role in the home. In 1860, *Godey's* circulation peaked at 150,000, making it one of the most widely read magazines in the country.

Right: A front cover of the *Lowell Offering*, which was written entirely by workers in their spare time after working long hours at the mill. The monthly magazine included poetry and fiction by the female laborers as well as articles on labor, religion, immigration, and slavery.

" DON'T BELIEVE THE OWNERS

"*Some say that 'Capital will take good care of labor,' but don't believe it; don't trust them. Is it not plain, that they are trying to deceive the public, by telling them that your task is easy and pleasant, and that there is no need of reform? Too many are destitute of [without] feeling and sympathy, and it is a great pity that they are not obliged to toil one year, and then they would be glad to see the 'Ten Hour Petition' brought before the Legislature. This is plain, but true language.*"

In 1846, the Female Labor Reform Association bought the *Voice of Industry* newspaper, and it became the voice of the female rebel mill workers who were fighting for better rights. In a letter from April 1846, the writer expresses distrust of the mill owners.

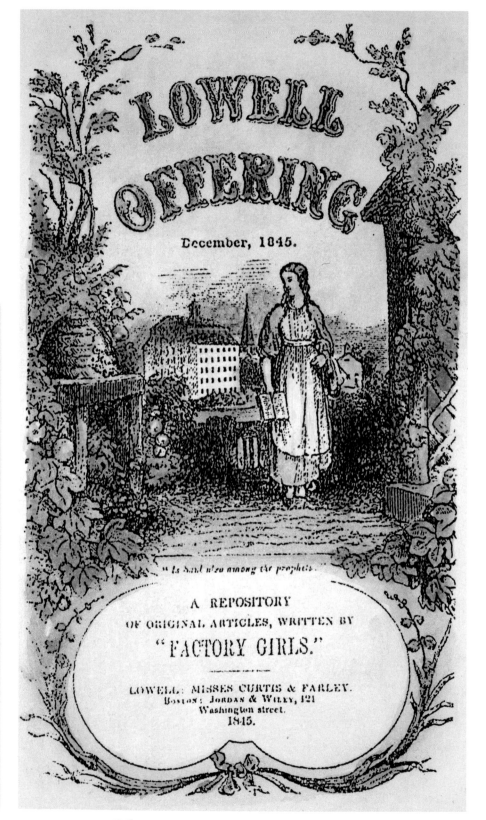

LOWELL OFFERING

December, 1845.

" *Is Saul also among the prophets.*"

A REPOSITORY
OF ORIGINAL ARTICLES, WRITTEN BY
"FACTORY GIRLS."

LOWELL: MISSES CURTIS & FARLEY.
Boston: Jordan & Wiley, 121
Washington street.
1845.

Right: Amelia Jenks Bloomer, founder of the *Lily*, who became better known for the bloomers outfit that she publicized in its pages.

A few publications reflected working-class women's lives. Female mill workers ran the *Lowell Offering* (1840–45), only accepting articles written by their colleagues. The magazine became well known, even outside the United States. The *Lowell Offering* also served the interests of the mill owners. It drew attention to their labor force and promoted the view that mill work was respectable. Despite being run by workers, the editorial policy was to defend the employers' reputation.

NEWSPAPERS PROMOTING WOMEN'S RIGHTS

Other publications promoted the developing women's rights movement. In 1829, writer and activist Frances Wright set up a radical newspaper called the *Free Enquirer* with socialist Robert Dale Owen in New York City. They argued for birth control and easier access to divorce to give women more freedom. Amelia Bloomer founded the monthly newspaper the *Lily* in 1849 after the Seneca Falls Convention. It supported women's rights and the temperance movement; Elizabeth Cady Stanton was a regular contributor under the name "Sunflower." The *Lily* lasted until 1856.

Established in 1853 by Paulina Wright Davis, the *Una* was a short-lived but influential newspaper "devoted to the elevation of woman." Topics included women's education, employment, and property rights. Paulina aimed to present well-educated women arguing the case for their rights in a respectable way. However, the newspaper was unable to attract enough subscribers and folded in 1855.

Women activists made good use of sympathetic newspapers such as the *Lily* and the *Una* and frequently wrote to others too. They also produced their own pamphlets to broadcast their message to a wide audience. Through their involvement in the media, women proved they could establish businesses, become successful writers, and offer more for female readers than fashion and fiction.

WOMEN OF COURAGE AND CONVICTION

PAULINA WRIGHT DAVIS (1813–76)

Born in New York, Paulina married merchant Francis Wright in 1833. The pair became active in the temperance, women's rights, and abolitionist movements. In 1835 they helped to organize an anti-slavery convention in Utica, New York, which led opponents to attack their home violently. Paulina then focused her attention on the women's rights movement, working with Ernestine Rose during the 1830s to petition for married women's property rights. Her husband died in 1845, but Paulina continued her reform work, taking the lead in organizing the national women's rights convention in Worcester in 1850. In 1853, she moved with her new husband, Democratic politician Thomas Davis, to Washington, D.C., where she established the *Una*. After the Civil War, Paulina worked tirelessly for the women's suffrage movement.

CHAPTER 8

THE PERIOD IN BRIEF

IN THE EARLY 19TH CENTURY, WOMEN WERE SECOND-CLASS citizens legally, politically, and socially. The ideology of separate spheres was widespread, although it did not apply to all sectors of society. By 1860, attitudes were beginning to change. In a few places, women had voting rights in their local area. For example, from 1838, widows in Kentucky with children aged six to eighteen could vote in school board elections. Over twenty states had expanded married women's property rights. Some states had made it easier to gain a divorce.

UNEQUAL LEGAL RIGHTS

"My legal position as wife deprives me of the power to use a cent of all the money I have earned, or may earn, only as I get it through a third person. I can[']t sell legally what I have acquired without Harry's [Henry's] consent. If I sign any transfer of his property I am ever insulted by being 'examined separately and apart from my husband' to know if it is by my own free will—my right to my name even is questioned and with all this smart, added to that I suffered as a woman, before I was a wife."

The Married Women's Property Act (1848) had improved married women's legal situation somewhat, but they still did not receive equal treatment. In 1857, Lucy Stone wrote a letter to Susan B. Anthony, expressing frustration about the loss of her legal rights on being married—which made her situation even more unequal than when she was single.

Right: A female college graduate in about 1860. Publicly funded education for girls expanded greatly in the early and mid-19th century and enabled a few women to attend college.

58

EDUCATION AND WORK

More girls and young women were attending elementary and secondary school and college, and the number of female teachers was growing—although extremely few had access to other professions. A minority of women now worked for wages outside the home. Women were increasingly joining charitable and reform societies that addressed problems in society.

WOMEN'S RIGHTS

The movement for women's rights was in a much stronger position in 1860 than it had been in 1828. Two generous Boston men, Francis Jackson and Charles Hovey, gave large donations to the women's movement in 1858 and 1859 so it could finance the meetings, lectures, and publications that were essential for it to move toward its goals. By 1860, women's rights activists were hopeful that they would improve their position in society and gain the right to vote. Indeed, women's suffrage was eventually granted in 1920.

Below: Elizabeth Cady Stanton (center, front row), Susan B. Anthony (second from left, front row), and many other women struggled for women's rights throughout their lives. By 1888, when this photo was taken, the movement had grown far stronger.

FIGHTING INCH BY INCH

"Speedily the State was aflame with disturbances in temperance and teachers' conventions, and the press heralded the news far and near that women delegates had suddenly appeared demanding admission in men's conventions; that their rights had been hotly contended session after session, by liberal men on the one side; the clergy and learned professors on the other; an overwhelming majority rejecting the women with terrible anathemas [detested things] and denunciations [statements of disapproval]. Such battles were fought over and over in the chief cities of many of the Northern States, until the bigotry [intolerance] of men in all the reforms and professions was thoroughly tested. Every right achieved: to enter a college; to study a profession; to labor in some new industry, or to advocate a reform measure, was contended [fought] for inch by inch."

In *The History of Woman Suffrage* (1881), Elizabeth Cady Stanton looked back on the struggle for women's rights since she and Susan B. Anthony had met in 1851.

Timeline

1790	The Second Great Awakening, a religious revival, begins.
1820s	The rise of the domestic novel, designed to appeal to women.
1821	Emma Willard opens the Troy Female Seminary in New York.
1823	Catharine and Mary Beecher found a girls' school in Hartford, Connecticut. It becomes the Hartford Female Seminary four years later.
1829	Frances Wright sets up a radical newspaper called the *Free Enquirer* with socialist Robert Dale Owen in New York City.
1820s–30s	Textile mills are constructed in the Northeast.
1820s–60	The building of elementary and secondary schools and colleges for boys and girls increases.
1831	Louis A. Godey establishes the magazine *Godey's Lady's Book*.
1832	The New England Anti-Slavery Society is founded. The Boston Female Anti-Slavery Society is formed. Mary A. Bathys founds the first women's anti-slavery organization in Salem, Massachusetts. Maria W. Stewart is the first African-American woman to speak out against slavery in public to audiences of men and women. Catharine Beecher opens the Western Female Institute in Cincinnati, Ohio.
	Native Americans from the Southeast are forced to resettle in Oklahoma. First Reform Act in Britain increases the number of men allowed to vote.
1833	The American Anti-Slavery Society is established in Philadelphia. The Philadelphia Female Anti-Slavery Society is set up. Slavery is abolished in the British Empire.
1836	Angelina Grimké publishes the anti-slavery book *Appeal to the Christian Women of the South*.
1837	The Anti-Slavery Convention of American Women, an inter-racial meeting, is held in New York City. The Grimkés lecture against slavery in New England. Mount Holyoke College, America's first women's college, is founded in South Hadley, Massachusetts. Oberlin is the first college to accept female students alongside men.
1838	Angelina Grimké presents an anti-slavery petition to the Massachusetts state legislature. Pro-slavery protesters attack the second Anti-Slavery Convention of American Women in Philadelphia. Widows in Kentucky with children aged six to eighteen are allowed to vote in school board elections.
1839	The American Anti-Slavery Society allows women to become full members. Abolitionist Theodore Weld publishes *American Slavery as It Is*.
1840	The World Anti-Slavery Convention takes place in London; women are not permitted to participate fully. Abby Kelley Foster is elected to the

business committee of the American Anti-Slavery Society.
Female mill workers set up the *Lowell Offering*.

1841	Catharine E. Beecher publishes *A Treatise on Domestic Economy*.
1844	Lowell mill workers form the Lowell Female Labor Reform Association.
1845	Margaret Fuller's book *Woman in the Nineteenth Century* is published. It argues for equality between the sexes.
1846	The Female Labor Reform Association buys the *Voice of Industry*, and it becomes the voice of the female rebel mill workers.
1847	Maria Mitchell discovers a new comet and becomes the first professional female scientist. The Factory Act in Britain introduces the ten-hour workday.
1848	The Seneca Falls Convention marks the start of the women's rights movement. The Married Women's Property Act allows married women to keep control of their property and rents and any profit they receive.
1849	Elizabeth Blackwell graduates as the first American woman doctor. Amelia Bloomer establishes the *Lily*, a newspaper for women.
1850	The first national women's rights convention takes place in Worcester, Massachusetts. The Female Medical College of Philadelphia opens. Maria Mitchell is elected to the American Association for the Advancement of Science, the only female member. Sojourner Truth publishes her autobiography.

1851	Elizabeth Smith Miller invents the bloomer outfit. Sojourner Truth makes an important speech at the Second Women's Rights Convention in Akron, Ohio. Maine becomes the first state to outlaw the production and sale of liquor.
1852	The Woman's New York State Temperance Society is founded. Harriet Beecher Stowe's novel, *Uncle Tom's Cabin*, is published.
1853	Antoinette Brown becomes the first American woman minister. Representatives from the New York State Temperance Society are refused admission to a meeting of the World's Temperance Convention. Paulina Wright Davis establishes the *Una*, a women's newspaper. Under the Gadsden Purchase, the United States pays Mexico $10 million for additional territory in southern Arizona and southern New Mexico.
1854	The Dress Reform movement ends.
1858	Lucy Stone refuses to pay tax on her property because she has no voice in the town government.
1858–59	Francis Jackson and Charles Hovey make large donations to the women's movement.
1859	J. S. Mill publishes *On Liberty*, which argues for basic freedoms in a democracy.
1860	The New York Married Women's Property Act allows married women to maintain their property separate from their husband's and to keep their own earnings.

Glossary and Further Information

abolitionist A person who fought for the abolition of slavery.

academy A school offering elementary and secondary education.

antebellum The period before the American Civil War.

bloomers An outfit consisting of a short dress worn over baggy trousers, adopted by some women in the early 1850s.

boardinghouse A house that provides rooms to rent and meals.

cholera A disease caught from infected water that causes severe diarrhea and can kill.

civil disobedience The refusal to obey particular laws or pay taxes, usually as a form of peaceful political protest.

convention A large meeting.

corset A piece of women's underwear that fits the body tightly and is worn to make the waist look smaller.

delegate A person who is chosen to represent the views of a group of people, for example, at a conference.

discrimination Treating a particular group in society unfairly, for example, because of their race or sex.

electoral To do with elections.

emigrate To go and live permanently in another country.

feme covert The legal situation of a married woman that meant her legal existence was incorporated into that of her husband. The married women's property acts of the 19th century started to grant some rights to women as individuals, separate from their husband.

humane Ensuring people do not suffer more than necessary.

ideology The set of ideas on which an economic or a political system is based.

immigrant A person who moves to settle in another country.

industrialization The development of industries.

Industrial Revolution The period in the 19th century in the United States when machines began to be used to do work and industry grew rapidly.

legislature A group of people who have the power to make and change laws.

literary critic A person who studies, evaluates, and interprets books.

lobby To try to influence politicians or the government to change a law.

Methodists Members of the Methodist Church, a Protestant Christian church. In the early to mid-19th century, it focused on establishing elementary and secondary schools and colleges and on missionary work.

missionary A person who goes to different communities or countries to teach people about Christianity.

petition A written document signed by a large number of people that asks somebody in a position of authority to do or change something.

plantation A large area of land where crops are grown.

preach To give a religious talk in church or another public place.

Puritans A Protestant Christian group that believed in worshipping God in a simple way and had strict moral attitudes.

Quaker A member of a Christian religious group that does not have formal Christian services and is opposed to violence. The Quakers were opposed to slavery.

racism Unfair treatment or violent behavior toward people of a different race.

reservation An area of land kept separate for Native Americans to live on.

resolution A formal statement of opinion agreed on by a group, usually by voting.

segregation The policy of separating people of different races (or religions or sexes) and treating them differently.

seminary In the early to mid-19th century, a school that focused on teaching girls domestic skills. Some seminaries taught academic subjects as well.

separate spheres The idea that women and men had separate roles in life. Women were responsible for the home and family while men dealt with work and other business outside the home.

slum An area of a city where the homes are in a very poor condition.

socialist A person who believes that everyone has an equal right to a country's wealth.

strike When workers refuse to work as a protest.

suffrage The right to vote in political elections.

suffragist A person who campaigns for the right to vote in political elections.

temperance Not drinking liquor because of moral or religious beliefs.

theology The study of religion and beliefs.

BOOKS

Crewe, Sabrina. *The Seneca Falls Women's Rights Convention.* New York: Gareth Stevens, 2004.

De Capua, Sarah E. *Great Women of Pioneer America.* Mankato, Minnesota: Compass Point Books, 2005.

Flanagan, Alice K. *Lowell Mill Girls.* Mankato, Minnesota: Compass Point Books, 2005.

Frost, Elizabeth, and Kathryn Cullen-Dupont. *Women's Suffrage in America.* New York: Facts On File, 2005.

Horn, Geoffrey Michael. *Harriet Tubman: Conductor on the Underground Railroad.* New York: Crabtree, 2009.

Kudlinski, Kathleen V., and Lenny Wooden. *Sojourner Truth: Voice for Freedom.* London, UK: Aladdin, 2003.

Lantier, Patricia. *Harriet Beecher Stowe: The Voice of Humanity in White America.* New York: Crabtree, 2009.

MacDonald, Fiona. *Women in History: 19th Century America.* Natick, Massachusetts: Chrysalis, 2003.

Marsico, Katie. *Lucretia Mott: Abolitionist and Women's Rights Leader.* Edina, Minnesota: Abdo, 2008.

Moore, Heidi. *Elizabeth Cady Stanton.* Portsmouth, New Hampshire: Heinemann, 2004.

Robbins, Trina. *Elizabeth Blackwell: America's First Woman Doctor.* Mankato, Minnesota: Capstone, 2006.

Stein, R. Conrad. *Harriet Tubman: On My Underground Railroad I Never Ran My Train Off the Track.* Berkeley Heights, New Jersey: Enslow, 2010.

Worth, Richard. *Teetotalers and Saloon Smashers: The Temperance Movement and Prohibition.* Berkeley Heights, New Jersey: Enslow, 2009.

DVDS

A History of Women's Achievement in America, DVD 1, Program 2: The Era of Women's Firsts, and DVD 2, Program 3: Women Speak Out (Ambrose/Video Center (2006).

WEB SITES

http://b-womeninamericanhistory19.blogspot.com/
www.chesapeake.edu/library/EDU_101/eduhist_19thC.asp
www.lkwdpl.org/wihohio/figures.htm
www.42explore2.com/suffrage.htm
www.kennesaw.edu/hss/wwork/index.htm